W9-AXC-874

J
796.6
Gut
Gutman
BMX racing

6408819
17.80

DATE DUE			

BMX Racing

Bill Gutman

Illustrated With Photographs
by Gork/ABA

Capstone Press

MINNEAPOLIS

Printed in the United States of America.

Capstone Press • 2440 Fernbrook Lane • Minneapolis, MN 55447

Editorial Director   John Coughlan
Managing Editor   John Martin
Production Editor   James Stapleton
Copy Editor   Thomas Streissguth

Library of Congress Cataloging-in-Publication Data
Gutman, Bill.
    BMX racing / Bill Gutman.
       p.   cm. -- (Action sports)
    Includes bibliographical references (p.) and index.
    Summary: Describes the beginning of motocross racing in the 1970s; the special bikes and tracks; the race with its turns, bumps, and passing; and the need for protective clothing. Includes a glossary of terms.
    ISBN 1-56065-262-4
    1. Bicycle motocross--Juvenile literature. [1. Bicycle motocross. 2. Bicycle racing.] I. Series
    GV1049.3.G88 1996
    796.6'2--dc20   95-7808
                                                            CIP
                                                            AC

99 98 97 96 95   6 5 4 3 2 1

Table of Contents

Chapter 1
BMX Racing

BMX means "bicycle motocross." If you like riding a bicycle fast, and if you like a good challenge, BMX racing may be the perfect sport for you.

You have to be an outstanding rider for BMX racing. You also have to be in top physical condition. You can't worry about an occasional bump or bruise. You are going to fall–usually when you and another rider collide.

Some riders prefer freestyle BMX–doing jumps, wheelies, and other tricks. There are freestyle contests, but a freestyle rider performs alone. He is judged only on his skill with his bike.

In BMX racing, you are going head-to-head against your opponents. It's a race to see who can cross the finish line first. You have to give everything you have for the whole race. You have to be competitive. You are racing to win.

How BMX Racing Got Started

BMX racing began in the early 1970s in California. Young bicyclists wanted to do more than just ride around on their bikes. So they began racing and doing tricks.

In 1970, a motorcycle movie called *On Any Sunday* showed motorcycles riding over rough terrain and flying high into the air. The movie gave some young riders the idea to make tracks with bumps and hills for bicycle racing.

The young riders quickly learned that their bikes just couldn't take the pounding. There were bent rims, broken spokes, and cracked **frames.** The riders had to try something different.

The BMX Bicycle

Soon bicycle manufacturers began to make a new kind of bike–the BMX bike–just for racing. With 20-inch (50-centimeter) tires, the bike was smaller and lighter than a regular street bike.

The BMX racing bike also had a very strong frame. The new bike was strong but light, and could go very fast. It could take the pounding a rider gave it, whether racing on a BMX track or doing freestyle tricks.

BMX bikes cost from about $100 for a basic model to $600 or more for a racing model. A bike that you buy at a shop is called a **stock bike**, no matter what the cost. Some racers like to customize or "trick out" their bikes. That means changing the bike to make it faster and better.

If you want to race, a good rule is to buy the best bike you can afford. Learn about it. If you want to make it better, buy better parts when you can. Before long, you will have a great racing bike.

Three BMXers take a jump near the finish of a heat.

The Track

BMX racers run on dirt tracks that are 800 to 1400 feet (240 to 420 meters) long. Most are level, but a few of the longer ones run downhill. The dirt on the track should be packed hard for better traction.

Even level BMX tracks aren't flat. They have jumps, bumps, and turns. A good track usually has one big jump and several smaller ones. Turns to both the right and left are called S-turns. Banks on the turns are called **berms**.

Most tracks also have a series of rounded bumps placed close together. These are called whoop-de-doos or **whoops**. Some big jumps have flat tops, called **tabletops**. Racers fly off the tabletops during a race.

It takes real skill to speed over these BMX tracks, especially in a close race.

Racers stay low to get maximum balance and speed.

Chapter 2
Your BMX Bike

BMX racers ride on that rugged track often. They will practice whenever they can. On race day, they will be out on the course in several heats, especially if they keep winning. So riders need to know their bikes very well, and they must be able to keep their bikes in top condition. Here are the important parts of a BMX bike and how to take care of them.

The Frame

The frame is made up of three metal tubes which are welded together. This part supports the rest of the bike and the rider. It must be strong, but light. Always check the frame for weak spots at the weld or any signs of cracks. If you see anything that doesn't look right, have it checked and repaired.

The Front Forks

The **front forks** are made of tubes, like the frame. They support the front wheel and must

Many BMX races are won on the final lap, when the racers are going full blast to the finish line.

Without wind and weather, indoor tracks allow the racers to go at a higher speed.

also be strong, but light. Check the forks for signs of wear and also for small cracks. Also make sure it is tight to the frame.

The Cranks

These are the metal arms to which the pedals are attached. The **cranks** and pedals drive the sprockets and chain. The longer the cranks, the more power you can get each time you pedal. Cranks sometimes must be tightened. If the ball bearings begin to make a grinding or rough sound, they're dirty. They need to be cleaned and greased again. Sealed bearings will not get dirty.

The Wheels and Rims

BMX bikes have either spoked or mag wheels. Spoked wheels are made of steel or aluminum. They are very light and usually used for racing. Mag wheels are made from a tough, molded plastic. They are heavier and tougher than spoked wheels, and used more often for tricks.

Check your wheels by turning the bike upside down and spinning them. If the wheels are not centered between the forks, they can be adjusted. If a wheel wobbles, you may have a bent rim. Sometimes the spokes need adjustment. A bike mechanic may be able to straighten the wheel. Or you may need a new wheel.

The Spokes

The spokes run from the center of the wheel to the rim. There is a trick to checking your spokes. Pluck each one like a guitar. You should hear a metallic twang. If you hear a dull sound, or if the spoke feels loose, it needs to be tightened with a spoke wrench. Don't make the spokes too tight–you may damage the wheel.

The Tires

BMX tires, or **knobbies,** are wide and have a deep tread. These tires can really grip a dirt track. They should usually be kept at the suggested air pressure. Some racers change this pressure a little. They like a softer tire on a hard track, and a harder tire on a loose track.

The Brakes

All BMX racing bikes have caliper brakes. Many racers like a brake on the rear wheel only. A front brake can be dangerous. A sudden stop with a front brake can send the rider flying over the handlebars.

A skilled rider can take the hills, berms, and S-turns without slowing down or losing position.

Always check the space between the brake shoes and the wheel. It should be the same on both sides–close but not touching. Make sure the shoes and cables are tight. To work well, the rubber shoes should not be too worn. They can be replaced easily.

Other Parts

There are other parts to be checked and maintained, too. The handlebars should be straight and tight. The chain should move up and down about half an inch (1.25 centimeter). It's easy to adjust the chain by moving the rear wheel backwards or forwards. Chains should be kept clean and oiled.

Pedals should spin free and easy. They should also be kept clean and oiled. The seat should be tight and set at the right height. The seat won't be comfortable, but racers don't sit much anyway. Hand grips should be tight and not spin, slip, or come off. Carefully clean and inspect your bike often.

Chapter 3

Getting Ready to Ride

Before you hit the track for the first time, there are two things you should do. First–and most important–get yourself in good shape. Second, learn and begin to practice some important safety measures.

Work Out First

Though BMX races don't last long, a rider must use a lot of energy. He may ride in several races in the same day, and he has to be as strong in the last race as he was in the first. The last race may well be the biggest race of the day.

You need to lean hard into the steeply banked turns known as berms.

A BMX racer must have strong legs and be able to pedal hard all the way through the race. He also has to have good endurance. A racer who is gasping for breath won't be able to pedal as hard as he wants. To get in this kind of condition, a racer should train by running or jumping rope.

Perhaps the best way to train is just to ride. You can practice by riding hard up hills. Or you can go for a long ride–sprinting for a distance, then riding easy, then sprinting again. This kind of training will work the leg muscles that you'll be using to race.

It also helps to strengthen other muscles by doing exercises like pushups, pullups, and situps. Also, make sure you eat right and get enough rest. A tired rider won't keep up with the competition and won't win. Do these things and you'll be in all-around good condition for race day.

Dress Right

BMX racers make sure that their bikes and their bodies are in top condition. To ride safely, they also dress right. They should wear protective clothing when riding and when practicing.

Anyone who competes in BMX racing is going to fall from time to time. You may collide with another racer, or lose control while going over a jump or a series of whoops. It can't be avoided. Serious injuries in BMX racing are rare, but you must be prepared anyway.

The most important piece of equipment is the helmet. Good helmets are made of strong fiberglass. They come in different colors and styles. There are two basic types–the open-face helmet and the full-face helmet.

The open-face helmet covers only the head. If you choose this style, you should wear a separate mouthguard. The full-face helmet covers the head, cheeks, chin, and mouth. It offers full protection. Both styles have padded liners and are held on by chin straps. Helmets are required in BMX competition at every level.

A good helmet costs $70 or more. It is well worth the price. Some come with visors attached to the front. A visor protects the rider's eyes from the sun and from dirt and small pebbles thrown up from the track. If you don't have a visor, you may want to wear a good pair of goggles. These will protect your eyes, too.

A full range of gear makes BMX racing a safe sport. Good riders are always ready for a spill or a collision.

More Protection

Always wear long pants and long-sleeved shirts. They protect you from scrapes and bruises–also known as road rash. Special padded pants have built-in pads on the hips,

knees, and shins. They also have tight legs. There are no chainguards on BMX racers, and loose pants can get caught in the chain.

If you don't want to buy the special pants, you can get your own pads. Knee and elbow pads can protect you from some bumps. Also, you can tuck your pants into your socks or put a rubber band around the bottoms. This keeps them clear of the chain.

High-top shoes are best, because they protect your ankles. They should have a tread so they won't slip off the pedals. Gloves will protect hands and wrists and give you a better grip on the handlebars.

Pad the Bikes, Too

Bike pads on the handlebars and crossbar (or top tube) can also protect you during falls. They are light and won't slow you down. The pads give you another little bit of protection.

Now that your bike and your body are ready, and you know all the rules of safety, there's only one thing left. It's time to race.

Chapter 4
Race Day

BMX racing has become a well-organized sport. There are several organizations that sponsor races and award trophies and other prizes. Riders are usually classified by their age, weight, and skill level. That way, you will always compete against other riders of similar skill.

There is a small registration fee the first time you ride. Racers get official number plates, which are mounted on the handlebars of the bikes. Sometimes a racer has to bring proof of his or her age. If you always race at the same track, the number and the registration fee are good for the entire season.

Before the race, official inspects all the racers' bikes. They want to be sure that there are no unsafe bikes racing around the curving, hilly tracks. Riders must also have helmets and any other protective clothing or gear that is required at that track.

A race is called a moto. There can be up to 100 races run in a day, with as many as eight racers in each. There are preliminary races called qualifying heats. These qualifying heats will eliminate slow and unprepared riders, leaving only the best racers in each class. Trophies are awarded for the final races.

Check the Track

It's a good idea for racers to check the track carefully before starting to race. Some like to walk around to see how hard or soft the dirt is. You can also check the turns, jumps, and whoops. If there are wet spots, or spots with a lot of small stones, you'll know. You can plan on the best place to pass, and where to put on that extra burst of speed if you need it. You can make a race plan in your head even before you start.

Next, you should loosen up to get ready for your first race. You might want to do some stretching exercises and a few jumping jacks to get your body ready for a sudden explosion of speed.

The Start

BMX races usually start from a raised

platform. A **starting gate** drops away to start the race, and a downhill ramp takes the riders onto the track. It is important for a racer to get a good start. It's easier to win when you are in front. If you start from behind, that means you have to pass others to win.

Good racers get up on both pedals as soon as they know the starting signal is just seconds away. Getting up fast gives them an advantage over riders who are keeping one foot on the ground. Strong first strokes that get you off the ramp fast are very important.

Starts can be practiced anywhere at any time. Just work to get the strongest first push on the pedals you can get.

Turns

There are ways to go around each different kind of turn on a track. Banked turns or berms are fast. Because the bike rides up on the berm, the rider can pedal through these turns as fast as he can. The bank keeps the bike from going out of control.

Some turns are too sharp to pedal around, even if they are banked. The experienced rider can slide around these turns at top speed. He or she puts a foot down for balance, makes a slide, and then starts pedaling again. To slide around a turn takes a lot of practice.

Flat turns can be tricky for a new rider. It might look as if you can pedal through, but without a bank, you can easily skid out. Good riders coast through part of a flat turn and then pedal when they feel they can.

It takes practice and experience to take turns well. At first, you will probably take them slowly and carefully . As you get better, you'll whip around the turns with the fastest riders on the track.

Bumps and Jumps

A big jump gives the rider a chance to show off his skill. He'll jump high in the air and twist his bike almost sideways before coming down. It might look great, but it won't help him win the race. On the big jumps, stay as low as you can. Go for distance, not height. Get the rear wheel back on the track and start pedaling.

On whoop-de-doos, use your judgment. A good rider can sometimes jump two or three at a time. But there is always the chance for a wipeout. If you go over them one at a time, you can usually keep your balance and keep pedaling.

In official races, riders compete against others with the same skill level. This makes the races close.

Always check the track for bumps and jumps before the race. Otherwise, you won't know what you're hitting, and that makes it tougher. If you walk the track first, you'll have a better idea how to take the rough spots.

Passing and Overall Strategy

It takes a lot of practice to pass on a track. There isn't much time or room, and everybody is making a dash for the finish line. That's why a good start is so important. But if you work up a fast speed, you'll have to pass slower riders in front of you.

Many riders like to pass on turns. Learning to take turns as fast as you can is part of becoming a champion racer. Most riders pick a spot or line on a turn and stick to it through the turn. If they take the high side or the low side, you have a chance to take the other line and try to get past.

On a banked turn, some riders will try to get up on the high side. Then they burst back down the bank to pass on the inside. Exploding off a banked turn takes skill.

On a straightaway, passing can be tougher. It takes leg strength and quickness. This is where that extra conditioning and good leg strength will help you.

A good racer will use his or her elbows and knees to keep others from passing. But hitting an opponent or cutting the other racers off with your bike is against the rules and may disqualify you.

Always look straight. Don't look from side to side or at other riders. If you take your eyes off the track, you might wipe out.

Wipe-outs

Everyone crashes from time to time. That's a fact of racing life. There aren't many serious injuries, but BMX racers do get scratches and bruises. If several racers are close together, there can be a chain accident. This happens when the first biker loses control, wipes out, and takes the racers behind down as well.

That's why safety equipment—helmets, protective clothing, and pads on the bikes—is important. A crash is called an **endo.** If you crash with no one near you, you can jump back on your bike and start up again. You may not win, but you won't quit, either.

Chapter 5
Organized BMX

Organized BMX racing, open to both boys and girls, takes place in many cities and towns. Race officials inspect bikes and enforce safety rules. They make sure there are no fouls or riding that can result in serious injury.

National organizations set rules and plan races. They find out the best racers from around the country and hold national

Tricks are fun, but good racers always stay in control. Flying into the air doesn't get you closer to the finish.

championships. They also award trophies and prizes to the winning riders.

By racing in regional and national contests, riders can make new friends and ride on new tracks. If you want to race, it's always good to test yourself with new challenges.

Form a Team

Sometimes riders get together and form a team. On a BMX team, it's a good idea to have riders in each class. A store, a local organization, or a bike shop can sponsor the team. The sponsor sometimes buys uniforms or trophies and helps racers keep their bikes in shape.

Even though BMX racing is an individual sport with one winner in each race, it's fun to be part of a team. You can train together, practice together, and help each other be better riders. You can also cheer for teammates who are racing in other classes.

If there are eight classes in an all-day race, and you and your teammates win six or seven of them, it's a great team victory. BMX racing is a great sport.

Glossary

berm–the banked part of the turn on a BMX racing course

BMX–letters that stand for "bicycle motocross"

crank-the two metal two arms to which pedals are attached

endo–a crash in BMX racing

esse–the turns on a BMX track

frame–the main part of the BMX bike, made of lightweight tubular steel or other metal

front fork–the part of the frame that holds the front tire

knobbies–tires with deep treads and knob-like projections for better traction

motos–the qualifying races at a BMX event

starting gate–the metal gate at the top of the starting ramp of a BMX racing track

stock bike–a bike with all the parts that came with it when it was new

tabletops–flat approaches to a jump on a BMX course

tricking out–changing original parts on a BMX bike to make it better and faster

whoops or **whoop-de-dos**–rounded bumps placed close together on the racing course

wipe-out–a crash on the BMX race course or while riding freestyle

To Learn More

Boulais, Sue. *Learning How: BMX Biking.* Marco, Fla.: Bancroft-Sage, 1992

Brimner, Larry Dane. *BMX Freestyle.* New York: F. Watts, 1987

Carstensen, Karol. *BMX Bikes.* Mankato, Minn.: Capstone Press, 1991

Sullivan, George. *Better BMX Riding and Racing for Boys and Girls.* New York: Dodd, Mead, 1984

Some Useful Addresses

American Bicycle Association
P.O. Box 718
Chandler, AZ 85244

Canadian BMX Association
1704 43rd Street
Vernon BC V1T 6W8
Canada

International Mountain Bicycling Association
Route 2, Box 303
Bishop, CA 93514

National Bicycle League
3958 Brown Park Drive, Suite D
Hilliard, OH 43026

Index